HEARTBEAT

Heartbeat

JILL BRISCOE

Harold Shaw Publishers
Wheaton, Illinois

ISBN 0-87788-340-8

Cover art copyright © 1991 by Victoria Hoke Lane

Library of Congress Cataloging-in-Publication Data

Briscoe, Jill.
    Heartbeat / Jill Briscoe.
        p.   cm.
    ISBN 0-87788-340-8
    1. Meditations. 2. Prayers. I. Title.
    BV4832.2.B73 1991
    242—dc20   91-24782
                                      CIP

---

99 98 97 96 95 94 93 92 91

10 9 8 7 6 5 4 3 2 1

To all the people
who intercede for us
regularly, diligently, faithfully.

Thank you
for the heartbeat
of your prayers.

Contents

Acknowledgments

We gratefully acknowledge the use of the following poems, previously published in other books by Jill Briscoe:

"Choosing to Be Chosen," "His Favorite Child" (in this book titled "My Favorite Child"), "That Calvary Be Worthwhile" (in this book titled "Heart Prayer"), and "Wings," in *Wings*. Wheaton, Ill.: Victor Books, 1988. Used by permission of the publisher.

"Hinds Feet," in *Running On Empty*. Dallas, Tex.: Word, Inc., 1988. Used by permission of the publisher.

"My Uniform," in *By Hook or By Crook*. Dallas, Tex.: Word, Inc., 1987. Used by permission of the publisher.

"Evergreen," in *Evergrowing, Evergreen*. Wheaton, Ill.: Victor Books, 1986. Used by permission of the publisher.

"Poor Mary!" and "Scourged My King," in *The Journey of a Disciple* (with husband Stuart). Ventura, Calif.: Regal Books, 1988. Used by permission of the publisher. Changes in "Scourged My King" © 1991 by Jill Briscoe.

My Heartbeat

My heartbeat is for marriage and the man in my life, Stuart—my other self, my husband and my friend—for whom I am personally thankful every day. He persuades me never to take myself too seriously. He brings the soft colors of love and laughter to my world and constantly challenges me to be the woman God made me to be. There has been no gray in our years together; rather ours has been a rainbow relationship, varied, rich, and colorful.

My heartbeat is for family, being best friends with our adult children and their spouses, yielding the dependency and control, but growing gold relationships between us like sunflowers, ever bright and cheery and oh, so beautiful. And of course, I want to be the perfect grandmother to all our grandchildren and other small eternal people yet to be born. I want to care about other people's families, too, and especially those who hurt and bleed and die a little bit on the inside every day because of the breakdown of their relationships. I do believe that God has answers for some and peace of mind for others when answers do not come, and that, one way or another, God, who thought up family in the first place, has the very best idea of how to bring sense to all the chaos of shattered dreams we see around us. I really believe that if I'm still and listen a lot, He will share some solutions with me so that I can share them with others.

My heartbeat is for women everywhere. Realizing so many of them feel inadequate, I count it all joy to encourage them into *doing* those things they never believed they could do, and into *being* the people they never believed they could be. Women are people made in His image, loved by the Lord, and I'm glad I can assure them of that.

Above all, my heartbeat is for God, and my great desire is this: to beat my heart into submission whenever it becomes hard or even lukewarm, so that it learns to die a little bit with sorrow when people need the Lord and they've no one to tell them about Him. I want to learn the tough lessons of life and overcome, so that I always have much to share and avoid sounding like a broken evangelical gramophone record.

Most of all I want my words to matter. Yet I know that words of wisdom that will make a difference have to come out of wise people, and there is no shortcut. I must start in the throne room with the Wise One, in His presence, before my words can ever march out into my world and be heard. So I know the best thing I can do for my world and for those I love is to be wise, fearing God, laughing at the devil, working my head off to see His kingdom come. I live for His honor, His principles, His smile, His people, and His work, because I love Him!

Jill Briscoe

Heart Prayer

*

Lord, where can we go but to Thee? We have no-one in
Heaven beside Thee, and no-one on earth with Your grand
ability to touch our spirits, lift our mood, bless our kids, stick
us back together again when we fall apart or sew a torn
relationship into place.

We wonder what You see in this wild world of ours
that we cannot.
A crowd of cowards?
A sea of sin?

A morass of people picking and clawing at each other? Hurt
husbands or rejected wives who find it difficult to look their
neighbors in the face? Or do You perhaps see those of us who
are celebrating? The "I have need of nothing" individuals, the
"keep your religion I have mine" group? The cynical or the
scoffer, or even little children capable of huge injustice on
their own sweet level?

See Lord, we are all here together . . . in this Thy hurting world
Have mercy on us all.

Nudge us into Your will and away from our wants . . .
Reduce us to size.
Show us Your Mighty Arm!
Carry our sin away
and move us into action
that we may make a bold stand
a walking statement that will tell
this needy world—
that Jesus is our public choice!

We pray this dear Lord,
that Calvary be worthwhile.

THE HEARTBEAT OF THE SPIRIT

Hinds Feet

*

The Sovereign LORD is my strength;
he makes my feet like the feet of a deer,
he enables me to go on the heights.
Habakkuk 3:19

Habakkuk's song of joy crowns a psalm of sorrow. In Psalm 22 Jesus is pictured as "the hind of the morning." At Calvary, the lion got the hind! But on Easter morning, the hind got the lion! He knows how to be surefooted on dangerous ground. He will help us be surefooted, too. We must remember the "high places" of spiritual experience are really the low places of life. He will give us hinds feet—when the time comes!

Hinds feet, give me Hinds feet, Lord—
like yours—

You are the Hind of the morning,
Walk with me on the heights
Help me to jump—to leap over the crevices—

You go first . . . show me how!
Land me safely on sure ground.

Give me a high view of Scripture
of the purposes and promises of God

Give me a vision from the heights of
the whole panorama of
your will and

Preserve me from the mountain lion
that would terrorize me.

Give me fleet feet—when the lion comes.
Yet and though he pounce and bring me down—
help me to bear it well.

And meet me on the other side of sorrow,
in a new place
in a new race,
in a new age, on a new page of
eternal history.

Until then, Oh Heavenly Hind of
the morning
Talk to me often about the dawn
of that new day!

Toughen me now—tenderly—
and give me . . . HINDS FEET!

Amen.

Wings

Give my words wings, Lord.
May they alight gently on the branches of men's minds
bending them to the winds of Your will.
May they fly high enough to touch the lofty,
low enough to breathe the breath
of sweet encouragement upon the downcast soul.

Give my words wings, Lord.
May they fly swift and far,
winning the race with the words of the worldly wise,
to the hearts of men.

Give my words wings, Lord.
See them now
nesting—
down at Thy feet.
Silenced into ecstasy,
home at last.

Generally speaking, I am frightened by my audience. Sitting on a platform, gazing out at a sea of faces, I hear myself introduced. I am the invited speaker, the one who has flown miles to be there with all these people who have invested their valuable time to hear me. I force myself through the intimidation barrier and search for a smiling face! I find one and eagerly fasten upon it. What encouragement! My eyes wander on finding a young adult—head bent, drooping shoulders—a beaten spirit. Next to her, two college-age boys gaze impudently at me: "Go on, impress us," they say without saying! Behind them sits a whole row of worldly-wise looking Yuppies. "Convince us," their body language demands. I think back to the dark morning hours. How glad I am at this eternal moment for the early call in the strange hotel that demanded that I tumble out of a strange bed to kneel on a strange floor with my most familiar Friend!

I know that if my words do not come out of my worship, I am wasting everyone's time. But they will—I have prayed my words will have wings—and they do!

Bare Feet

*

*"Take off your shoes, for this is
Holy ground."*

"All right, Lord, I understand.
You can't wash my feet if I'm
wearing sin's sandals.
See!—bare feet!
I'm standing still now—
on Holy ground.
Somehow it's hard to trample
all over other people's lives
with bare feet, Lord.

"I feel awkward like this
dressed, yet naked—humbled—
Bare feet!
Funny things—
but ready to be shod

with the gospel shoes
You would give me to wear.

"But first, Lord—
—wash me—!"

The Pharisee in Me

*

Thoughts from Matthew 5:3-11

One day I found within my heart
someone who'd been there from the start.
A prudish person—self appointed,
self sufficient—self anointed.
Though I, a true disciple be
I've met the Pharisee in me!

*Blessed are
the poor in
spirit*

Oh, Lord, I pray hard on my way
I try to do it every day
A publican to be I try
and beat my breast and sigh and cry
I'm hoping others round will see—
oops—there's the Pharisee in me!

*Blessed are
those who
mourn*

He sees not why his heart should bow.
Instead he's holier than thou.
He casts the mote out of your eye,
while beam in his obscures the why

a tear be shed because of sin
or why he should begin again.
Forgive me, Lord, the sin you see,
I've met the Pharisee in me!

Blessed are
the meek

He's there as I start out my week
advising me that meek is weak.
he's up before me every day,
to figure out a better way
than following Him submissively.
I've met the Pharisee in me!

Blessed are
those who
hunger and
thirst for
righteousness

He tells me, "Oh, you know enough
just keep on with the same old stuff—
you've books galore and tapes to lend,
you've Christian magazines to send.
No need to learn theology—"
I've met the Pharisee in me!

Blessed are
the merciful

He passes people every day
Who've lost their innocence some way.
He says a prayer for those poor fools,

for breaking his religious rules
"No time for mercy now," says he,
"at Bible study I must be."

Blessed are the pure in heart

He laughs when told of a pure heart,
And wants no parcel or no part
of looking in and seeing sin
when such a perfect man he's been.
He spends his life in holy work
and never quits and never shirks.
He shines the outside of his cup,
and knows not that he'll finish up
in dungeon deep, in hell's abyss—
cause God condemns a man like this!

Blessed are the peace-makers

The father reasons with the son
that mercy and forgiveness won . . .
the offending brother be restored
that retribution be outlawed,
that loving welcome be extended,
instead the Pharisee's offended.

He wants the boy to crawl, you see,
I've met the Pharisee in me.

Blessed are those who are persecuted because of righteousness

The Pharisee reviles the one
who tries to follow God's dear son.
He persecutes the witness who
confesses Christ his whole life through.
He murders life when e'er he finds
disciples who with peace of mind,
refuse to cower or bow the knee,
to him—the Pharisee in me.

I know the Lord rebukes my guest
in scathing words, at God's behest.
He tells me "heed his words of strife
and realize he saps your life."
He hates to share my heart, you see,
with him, the Pharisee in me.

And why should He the God of grace
be forced to live here face to face
with him who hung Him up to die

against an angry, anguished sky—
who pierced His feet and crowned His head,
who laughed, and left Him very dead?
Forgive me, Lord, I beg of Thee,
deal with the Pharisee in me!

The beautiful attitudes Jesus taught in the Sermon on the
Mount are opposed by the old nature—the flesh—the
Pharisee in me. May we walk after the Spirit and ignore the
old man, so experiencing true joy.

————————

Oh Lord, we pray for eyes to see
a judge who's fair, a Trinity
who'd have us lay our bias down
and quit the prejudicial frown.

When we're in heaven and take our place
and look for some familiar face
and realize He's long
accepted

the people who
we've long rejected

Then help us not to make a fuss
when we see they're not
expecting us!

Amen!

Prayer

*

Lord, forgive us for our huge ability to see the faults
in others before we see our own.

Our eyes—so full of planks of prejudice prevent us
not
from seeing minute motes
of little account
within our brother's eye.

Guilty as charged, we proudly pronounce
—and they may well be—
But oh, dear Lord, what right do we
small measly mortals
have to judge the motives
of men's hearts?

Teach us that there be but one
great throne of judgment and
that it be most thoroughly
occupied by Thy dear self.

And may we through the knowledge of Thy Son
demolished by our sense of
sinfulness
so know our jungle natures' tendencies,
we are forced to cry, "Oh God, be merciful to 'me,'
a sinner!"

And may the tolerance that
mercy births
precipitate a caring of the heart
producing prayers
set free from
judgment chains that change a
world—
our world!
Our troubled, tumbled, truculent, terrible,
tantalizing, touching world!

A world of moms and dads and little ones
fighting for their families—
Oh, may they win!
Hold them together, Lord,
Hold them fast,

prevent them from blowing up their lives
with the devil's dynamite.

Give us grace to tell them—Jesus makes the
difference!

Amen.

My Uniform

*

I see you smiling while I strip my
clothes of comfort off,
I hear you laugh as water splashes
in the bowl,
I look above and catch Divinity's
delight,
I kneel and seek with washing word
to cleanse a soul.

Yet, I could never dare to dress in
servant's garb
Unless I first have known Your
cleansing blood,
Have fallen prostrate, crying—
"Mercy, Lord . . .
forgive my filthy feet their
wayward road!"

So humble this high head
till low it bows,

Before the cross where sacred head
hangs low,
Teach me the lowly secret of
the Christ
Then help me hear You say . . .
"My servant—go."

Oh, Lord—may I be known by my
uniform—
the towel!

We were on the outskirts of Manila in the Philippines, visiting
a missionary couple. We walked on Smokey Mountain.
Smokey Mountain is just that—a smoldering rubbish heap on
the surface of which people actually live—if you can call it
that! Slums like this are among the worst in the world. We
walked down the putrid streets with our friends. These
missionaries belonged to "the order of the towel," as we call it.
Both were young people, highly qualified in their professions
in the West. Both had chosen to bring their three young
children to live near Smokey Mountain so they could wash

feet. "I like being here," said the young mother simply. I didn't doubt her. We knew she meant it. Her eyes shone, and her compassionate touch with the people proved her free of hypocrisy. The young husband was helping to catch a pig an elder of the church had lost. The church was right there in the very heart of the slum, next to the open sewer that floods over the ramshackle shacks whenever it rains. A church full of people Christ died for and sent His servants to love and nurture. That night in our lovely, clean hotel room, I thought of Jesus stripping to the waist and washing the disciples' feet, and then I thought of our young friends. After that I prayed, "Oh, Lord, may I be known by my uniform—the towel!"

Jesus, Jewel of Heaven

*

To know Christ is to be rich beyond measure, wealthy beyond your wildest dreams. After all, Jesus is the Jewel of Heaven! Let me tell you a story.

He was the Richest Man in the Valley. There was no disputing it. Secure and confident, he was escorting his house guests to their expensive cars, when John, his gardener, cap in hand, approached him to give him a message. The man was poor and shabbily dressed and looked embarrassed to be talking to the Richest Man in the Valley. He shuffled from one foot to the other.

"Well, out with it, man," his employer snapped impatiently, his eyes on his departing guests.

"Sir," John stuttered. He was obviously *very* nervous.

"Sir—I know this sounds mighty strange, but I had a dream last night that really upset me. I dreamt that the Richest Man in the Valley would die tonight at midnight! You all right, sir?" he finished lamely, feeling exceptionally stupid.

His boss stared at him. John was all right as gardeners go. He worked hard and was honest and trustworthy, but the Richest Man in the Valley was aware that he attended the little evangelical church in the village and was one of those "born-again Christians." He'd never had much time for religion himself, always felt too much church made you a little weird. John's words confirmed his suspicions! "You don't need to worry about me, John," the Richest Man in the Valley said impatiently and cheerfully, turning on his heel.

John watched him disappear inside the huge carved door of the mansion and felt relieved. It had taken all of his courage to talk to the man, but the dream had been so sharp—he'd never experienced anything like it. Had God sent him a message in his dream, he wondered? He worried about the Richest Man in the Valley. He had no idea where he stood with God.

The Richest Man in the Valley closed the door of his beautiful home and looked around. Silly to let the poor man's words bother him. Why, things had never been better. It wouldn't do any harm, though, he mused, to invite his doctor round for a drink—late in the evening!

So, late that night the Richest Man in the Valley and his doctor enjoyed a game of cards and talked at length about world affairs and the stock market. The clock on the expensive wooden panelling ticked on: five minutes to midnight, four minutes to midnight, three minutes, two minutes. One minute—MIDNIGHT! Irritated with himself that he felt so relieved, the Richest Man in the Valley bade the doctor goodnight and retired. He had no sooner climbed into bed than the doorbell rang urgently. Hurriedly wrapping his robe around him, the Richest Man in the Valley ran downstairs to answer the frantic knocking.

A young girl stood on the doorstep, her eyes red with weeping. Her clothes were old, and she carried what looked like her mother's purse.

"What's the matter?" the Richest Man in the Valley inquired, not unkindly.

"Sir," she gulped, "I just came to tell you that tonight at midnight my father died."

"Your father? Who is your father?" asked the puzzled man.

"John," the little girl replied softly, tears coursing down her face. "John, your gardener—the RICHEST MAN IN THE VALLEY!"

To know Christ is to be rich beyond measure, wealthy beyond your wildest dreams. For after all . . .

Jesus is the Jewel of Heaven!

THE HEARTBEAT OF LIFE

Word of God

*

Oh, Word of God
Pound on my soul,
Drench my life and make me whole.

Accomplish that for which you came,
sprinkle my way
with gentle rain.
And if sometimes the Word seems cold,
help me to read
though it feel old,
for ice and snow can melt
with spring,
and in God's time change everything!

Oh, Word of God
produce in me—
a bud—a flower—who knows—
a tree.
A gentle shade for
those in need,

A place where hungry ones can feed.
A watered
garden
I would be—
Oh, Word of God—
rain Thou on me!

Generic Christians

*

Stimulated by standing in line at a checkout counter, looking at all the generic products

Fervency is a
fighting fervor, that saves us
from being
GENERIC Christians;

Believers without a patent;
plain, colorless
with no distinctive
markings
on our lives.
Generic disciples settle for a cheap faith,
a
passable Christianity—

People who say that their type of faith will do! But when
they are asked

"What" it will do—they are hard put to
answer!

Fervency refuses to buy the idea of
generic faith,
determining rather to spend more
whatever the cost
in terms of ardor and effort
to purchase a brand of belief
that has the unmistakable
"quality" of fervor
about it.

Hot, exciting power
that insists on
faith being more than

minimal involvement
content
with a
passing
grade!

After all the "fervent effectual prayer of
a righteous
man
availeth much"

While generic ineffectual prayer of
righteous men availeth
little or nothing at all.

Fervent faith is a daily choice for the follower of Jesus.
It marks a man or woman out from the
generic pack
It makes us want to be like Him
—
JESUS WAS NOT GENERIC!

In the words of an outrageous song
"they don't make Jews like Jesus
anymore!"

Perhaps the world believes
God doesn't make *anyone* like Jesus anymore

because
of
us!

O Lord
Make us like
Your Son

Fervent lovers of God
Daring to be
different

Show us the way to be—
name brand
Christians;

Patented with colorful
markings—

branded with a logo peculiarly
shaped like a
cross.

Generic Christianity will never win the world
for Christ

But fervent faith will!

Sunday School

*

Patience doesn't mean being patient with disobedience, but rather patiently seeing the thing required is done—like attending Sunday school.

Sunday school was always a priority for our children. We "all" went. This showed them it was important for us, too—that helped. Sunday school was put before sports, friends, parties, homework, T.V., and sleep. That's what "priority" means—putting something first, not last.

It's hard work—but worth it. I never had the privilege of going to Sunday school. When I found Christ, I made the Lord a promise. If He ever gifted me with the priceless gift of a family, I would make sure Sunday school was a priority. Three kids and five grandkids (at the present count) later, I can tell you it paid off. I overheard our eldest son, David—a pastor now—patiently explaining to his four little ones how important Sunday school was and how it was a family priority, and I thanked God that he's obviously intent "on growing good children 'replete' with the likeness of their Maker!"

Love works hard to make truth clear
as crystal, easy to understand.
Love believes in Sunday school
in little minds needing little lessons—
about a big God
Love gently instructs those it
loves to accept truth's tenets,
ancient values, moral codes.
Love hopes for a ready response
but makes allowances for
human frailty
Love trusts twice, forgives freely
while expecting the best.
Love is ever patient
using time
to grow a good child,
replete with the likeness of its Maker.

A Prayer for Missionaries

✳

A world of poverty and famine
Of people living hand to mouth
in desperate straits,
in economic nightmare,
needs to find some present help today.

We pray for missionaries.
These special servants, Lord.
We ask for a freedom
from their own peculiar
bias of Christian cultural heritage.

A mighty moderation
that becomes a bridge for Jesus
to use on His way
through their hearts
to His hurting world. Amen.

Hot Water

*

Am I like a tea bag
waiting to know, what flavor I am
when in hot H20—?

Am I like a tea bag
soggy and wet?
Am I asking the Lord
just how hot it can get?

I want to be able
to give out for sure
a fragrant aroma
that makes folks want more.

But that means hot water
that hurts my deep pride,
that cleans out my life
till I'm tired inside,
of a fragrant-less life
that knows not how to sing—

So dip me in water,
but keep hold of the string!

Sometimes we don't know what fragrance is inside of our lives till the Lord dips us in hot water! But then that can be cold comfort when it happens. "Why should this particular trouble have come looking for me?" I complained one day. "Why shouldn't it?" retorted a friend. "Why should we Christians be exempt?" Why, indeed!

Hot water causes the sweet aroma of Christ to be released. Remember that little tea bag the next time trouble boils up around you!

A Prayer about Work

*

Father, we thank You for the dignity You afford us in providing us with work, and we praise You for the "value" we feel in being able to provide for our families. We thank You, too, for the ability You have given many of us to create work opportunities for other people, that they may feel their intrinsic worth as well.

We thank You that You worked creating Your marvelous universe, and that Christ, Your Son, labored at a carpenter's bench while visiting Your planet. Because of this we know You understand us, and that You are aware of the many problems that arise because of our wayward and lazy natures.

Help us to be like You. May integrity matter to us; may respect for others be grown in the soil of our lives till it generates trust in those who watch us work. May we be truthful in our dealings with others, and deliver us, dear Lord, from greed and avarice. Teach us to put a premium on the things that really matter—like life and health, marriage and family love, and the privilege of giving. May our position of influence that You have entrusted to us be used and not abused.

Amen.

Ordinary People

*

There are, in fact, no "ordinary" people where God is concerned.
Thinking about this one Christmas, I was reminded that the God
of love chose shepherds—men on the bottom of the totem pole
in their society—to be treated to a rendition of the "Messiah" by
the heavenly host and to be given the privilege of being the world's
first missionaries! That prompted a poetic response.

Love never paints
an unfinished sunset

Or makes half a world or a
bird with one wing.

Love always completes the things
He starts.

One day it will all be over and
we will be like Him, but
till then—
Love affirms the loved one

with words
refusing to let silence
punish an offender.

Love isn't afraid to
tell the truth
or face the facts
or level—
but always in love, of course.

Love delights to use ordinary people—
To help people who don't
realize how loved ordinary
people are!

Teachers and friends,
and even parents
insist we discover we are
special;
after all, they tell us,
God thought we were worth
dying for!

Evergreen

*

Blessed is the man
who does not walk in the counsel of the wicked
or stand in the way of sinners
or sit in the seat of mockers.
But his delight is in the law of the LORD,
and on his law he meditates day and night.
He is like a tree planted by streams of water,
which yields its fruit in season
and whose leaf does not wither.
Whatever he does prospers.
Psalm 1:1-3

O Lord, I'd bear some fruit for Thee
If I could just stand still
And let my roots grow deep and wide
Entwined around Thy will.
I'd need to learn to wait for Thee,
To whisper to my heart;
I'd have to let the Holy Ghost
Have all, not just a part.

The problem, Lord, I have is this,
I cannot stand quite still;
Too many other neat tree friends
Are planted on my hill.
I feel a little guilty
But I've only me to thank;
I'm far too busy rushing
Up and down my river bank.

There's Myrtle, Rose, and Holly
Who are friends of mine, you know;
We're so busy having fellowship,
We have no time to grow.
They're the cutest little saplings,
The sweetest things to nurse,
There's little time to meditate
On chapter and a verse.

Now I've grown to be an expert
On blight and stunted trees,
So I run extensive seminars
With spiritual expertise.

I tell willows not to wallow
And chestnuts not to crack,
So I'm far too tired to watch and pray
By the time that I get back.

O Lord, don't chop me down
And use my trunk for firewood;
I'd love to stop my frantic pace
And settle, if I could.
Take hold my tree and planteth me;
Don't let my green leaves wither.
Oh, let my thirsty branches drink
Cool water from Thy river.

Dear King of forest glades and glen,
O tree King, I adore Thee;
I'll take root where I am planted,
Content to bring Thee glory.
O Spirit, cause my leaves to shine,
True fruit at last be seen,
I yield to Thee—Oh, touch my tree
And keep me evergreen.

THE HEARTBEAT OF THE SEASONS

Relinquishment

＊

Judy was getting married. How ever could my "little" girl be ready for such a "big" step, I wondered. I reminded myself that clutching crushes love, and then I shut my eyes and thought about Jesus gently taking my hands that were holding tightly onto my daughter and loosening their grip. "You're not losing the relationship—just the dependence upon it," He reminded me. A few years later, my married little girl (she'll always be "my little girl," I suppose) wrote about our mutual struggles to give each other "space to breathe and room to grow." We both penned our thoughts, and a book was born. When the chapter on relationships was finished, I concluded it with this poem.

Relinquishment doesn't grab or clutch.
Clutching crushes love;
Love can't breathe easily
when it's controlled
by possessive
hands.
Trust grows best

when it's planted in
respect.
It flowers in profusion
when joys are shared.
Letting go is a learned art—
Jesus is the best
teacher.
I need to be the best pupil.
Love will help me
let go—
if I ask Him to.

A Mother with Baby

*

A mother with baby
thanks God every day
that a small living person
has come here to stay.
God's chosen her family
to teach them of love
and the care of their Father
in heaven above.

A mother with baby
is filled with such joy
for she's nursing an infant,
a girl or a boy, who's
eternal, though tiny and
able to know
a God who redeemed them
a long time ago.

A mother with baby
prays over the bed

where her little one lies
when he's bathed and he's fed,
and she knows the Lord
hears at the end of the day—
and she gives Him her fears
that her child find the way.

Then a mother with baby
feels God in her heart
Assuring her gently if she'll
do her part . . .
He'll care for her baby as He
cared for His Son—
For the Father's full giving
is only begun!

The Mooring Post

*

Little one, safe harbored now beyond
thy stormy journey into birth,
Little one wrapped warmly in the
smiles of God that brought
thee to this earth.
Now tethered to the
mooring post of parents who
employ
their grand and privileged
guardianship of
thee—their
little boy!

Parents are intended to be a mooring post, a safe place to stay,
a sure place to cast anchor come wind or weather. It is not the
time to worry about the storms beyond the bay, for now we
have the gift of a little time called childhood; tethered to love,
the little boat bobs and weaves about the post—happy and
secure!

Gold Faith

*

for child dedication

Dear Father,
Whose very nature is to care,
see us here,
Your own forever family,
Suspended in time and space,
turning our thoughts toward
Thee.

Dear God,
Whose very nature is to love,
So fan the flames of all our
family relationships,
that they may be a warm place
where children love to play,
where people live to give each other
room to breathe and space to grow.

Dear Lord,
Whose very nature is to give,
Teach us what that means,
That Jesus, Savior of our lives
may lend His power
of giving
to our selfish hearts.

Almighty One,
Whose very nature is to overcome,
We fear the forces
marching on our homes
with cruel intent to harm us.
We peep behind the drapes of dread
drawn tight across our future dreams
and shudder at the menace of man's ways.

We know not what to do!
Fight Thou for us.
You are our Mighty Conqueror!

Protect our little ones and lend us
weaponry to reinforce our souls with

muscles of Your might—
faith—
hope—
and love.

And oh, dear Teacher,
so show us how to model Christ in all His
sweet simplicity and strength . . .
that seeing Him in me, my children shall inherit
Gold faith! —
Trust, tried in the crucible of life,
my gift to them—
a godly heritage.

Amen.

Favorite Child

*

I wanted to be God's favorite child—until I began to think about it. Then I wasn't so sure. I read, "This is my Son, whom I love; with him I am well pleased" (Matthew 3:17). And then: "He himself bore our sins in his body on the tree" (1 Peter 2:24a). After that I wrote the Father a letter.

"I want to be Your favorite child, Father!"

"You do?"

"Yes, I really do. That sounds like fun!"

"My favorite child like who?"

"Well, like Jesus."

"Then flatten out your hands upon My cross,
Pile foot on foot that nails may stave them in.
Hang high, hang long above the blood-soaked turf

And bear my judgment deep upon your soul for others' sin.
Then, go to hell, my child, my favorite child!"

"Oh, that doesn't sound like too much fun after all."

This heavenly conversation taught me to pray about the costly "privileges" of being a "favored" son of God.

——Prayer for Students at Commencement——

*

Oh God,
As I commence to commence,
I ask three things—
Firstly, that my knowledge of Thee
far exceed my knowledge
of all other things!
Make me a walking statement
of Thy Word,
that those that won't read, must read,
and reading, learn the old, old
story—purely told till I am old,
and come to Heaven
to read Thee there
without a book or page between us then
but face to face
Oh, joy!

And then, I ask my service for thee
far exceed my service of all
other things.

Make me a walking statement
of Your power,
that serving I delight Thy heart and see Thy smile.
That what I "am" bring glory to Thy name.
And what I do be secondary—
to this higher goal!

And then, again, I ask Thee
that my love for Thee
so far exceed my love
for ought else—
person, ambition, joy,
or crown.
Make me a walking statement
of Thy love that
those who won't love
must love
for love begets itself!

Oh, Lord of my commencement,
set my course and
journey with me now

through the life
You have planned for me
that only can spell full fulfillment.

Amen.

THE HURTING HEARTBEAT

— A Prayer for Sick Children Everywhere —

*

O God, You are the heavenly Parent,
The One who as a Father watched Your
child upon the cross and
heard His cry for comfort.

Those of us who believe in You
know You as a suffering
God, and so can lean our
heads upon Your breast and say:
"It helps to know—
You know."

Oh God, You are the compassionate Helper,
touched by the very feelings
of our infirmities you say:

Help those of us that want to help, to learn the art of saying
the right thing—that those
of us who do not have a

60

tongue of silver may through your inspiration
make rich those who
know the poverty of
bodily health.

And You who are the One in heaven that
revealeth secrets—that shows men the
mysteries of medicine;
roll away the stone from "this" grave
and show the doctors secrets of
the resurrection—
life—from death!

Oh God, You are the Healer . . .
The Helper
the Hearer of your children's cries:
Presence yourself with us
and care for the little ones we
know you love
and died for.

Amen.

Love Listens

*

Love listens—using silence to talk
louder than a thousand words—
bending near the sick one,
focusing attention
on the need.

Looking as though there's
no one else in the
wide, wide
world
Except the one who needs to talk.

Love is watertight, never leaking
the confidences shared at midnight—
or at dawn—or in the middle
of the day!
Time is irrelevant to love.

Love borrows wisdom from on high
passing on eternity's

information
at the right time and in
the right way.

Love's ears are open to a shriek
or groan, complaints or
angry shout.
It matters not—
love listens.

Talk to Him—
you'll see,
and you'll be back again,
No one listens
like Love!

Today

*

Today the pain is not too bad, and I'm
grateful . . .
That's good! Today will be a good day.
I will greet friends,
work on work,
cook a little,
laugh a lot,
watch my favorite basketball team on TV.

I will plan for the next ten hours ONLY—
but carefully—
trying to pack the precious
moments with right
things to do.

Today is going to be quite achievable . . .
Tomorrow may not be like this.
But, hallelujah, "then" is not "now,"
and I don't need to live it yet.

I am glad!

Thank you, Jesus.

Amen.

Jesus:
"Therefore do not worry about tomorrow,
for tomorrow will worry about itself."
Matthew 6:34a

The Widow

*

When we were small, Mother used to have an endearing habit
of bending over my sister Shirley and me, patting her round,
smooth cheek, and demanding, "Kiss me here!" We loved to
obey her order. I caught my breath as I found myself repeating
the very same ritual with my own grandchildren some fifty
years later. What small kisses mean to the heart! Yet never
more is this the case than when the mother or grandmother is
a widow. Then the kiss of a child becomes heaven's breath of
sweet encouragement, a reminder of a belonging that only
"family" can bestow. A necessary solid token of life in the
sinking sands of sorrow. A little one's kisses are the very best
medicine for bereavement!

As feather to bird on high
as rain is to a cloud,
as light to angels' wings in heaven
as laughter laughed out loud;
as leaf to tree and leg to knee
as clear brook to the hart—

are children to the widow
and kisses to her heart!

As sunshine to the winter earth
as frogs are to a pond,
as shooting star to galaxy
as planet to beyond
as kitten to a dish of milk
and horse to rope and cart—
are children to the widow
and kisses to her heart!

As baby is to mother's breast
and hearth to wandering man,
foundations to a building
and pancakes to a pan,
as hairspray is to hair and curl
and dartboard is to dart—
are children to the widow
their kisses to her heart!

Right to Life Day

*

Right to Life Day was coming up. The worship committee asked me to offer a prayer in the morning service. I thought about the first time I'd held Daniel David, our first grandchild, in my arms. "You are so clever," I told the "kids" (our adult children). "With God's help you've managed to make a little eternal person!" He was so tiny, so helpless, and though he didn't know it then, so glad his parents had given him the chance to know the Christ we knew and to live forever! It was Christmas time, so it was easy then to think of Joseph and Mary's dilemma. Without their right decision, none of us would live forever.

Some 2,000 years ago, Joseph son of Jacob, faced
with an unwanted pregnancy, had it in mind, in order
to avoid public disgrace, to put her away privately—
"Mary," I mean.

If Joseph had been faced with that unwanted pregnancy
in the 90s, he might have had it in mind to—
take "it" away privately—
the fetus, I mean!

Just think—
then there would have been:
no Savior
no forgiveness
no hope of heaven
no One to listen to our prayers . . .
no Jesus!

Whatever would have happened to us
if someone had
aborted Jesus!

Yet Jesus said,
"As much as ye have done it unto
one of the least of these,
ye have done it unto me!"

Lord, forgive us . . .

Prayer for Life

✳

Lord, we pray for men and women reaching out for life—
Your life You say: with knives, coat hangers, and worse.
Show them that they are killing small, eternal people.
We pray for babes unborn who have no way to pray themselves—
for chance to raise their voice in praise,
to taste the endless days that Grace affords.

We pray for little ones who'd say to us,
"Please let me be a person just like you—
Oh, let me have a Christmas, too, so I can hear about the Christ
Who came like me,
unwanted by the many, loved by few—
to die at Calvary."

Lord, set our hearts toward these issues of our day
grow up our consciences
until they stand adult and ready for the way:
armed for battle, suited for defense—
Your soldiers!
For Jesus' sake, Amen.

The Place of Beginning Again

*

When all you have left is commitment
When all that remains is the ring
that fastens you into a marriage
that somewhere forgot how to sing;
When babies, business, or boredom
Take the tenderest moments away,
when all you have left is commitment
it's high time you started to pray!

When all you have left is commitment,
when your differences make you aware
that relating's too much of a struggle,
so silence is easier to bear;
When you're locked into grim nonalignment—
with no one to help on the scene,
and you helplessly look at the future
regretting the past that has been.

Yet you're Christians—that's why you're together—
you promised that right from the start

for better or worse, you'd be partners
till death, not divorce, did you part;
So when all you have left is commitment
in name only you're husband and wife,
ask Jesus to breathe on your marriage—
that's why he came into your life!

For commitment's the altar of marriage
where the sacrifice starts to be made—
but love is the flame that ignites it,
that laughs at the price to be paid.
So Lord, place your nail-pierced hands 'round us,
fan the hope that is dying to flame,
and remind us the reason for Calvary—
it's the place of beginning again.

Overtaken with Joy

*

Isaiah 35:10

Years ago a young man we met on the streets of Europe found
Christ. A few months later he stood up to testify to his
newfound faith. "I've been running away from God for years,"
he said, "but I discovered He has longer legs than I have!"
This was the incident that I "married" to this meditation.

Sorrow would bury us
because sorrow is the undertaker.
Joy is Jesus—Jesus is
the Overtaker
who overtakes the undertaker
and
dresses our spirit in
a garment of praise!

Joy is Jesus—God in
Galilean cloth

touching our lives—
offering us life!
And making our hearts smile.

Don't try to run away
from the Lord—
Remember He has longer legs than you have!

Unanswered Prayer

*

Tender Jesus, caring for the ones who
care not anymore—
For those beaten by circumstances
and driven by sorrow
to believe that
they are lower than dogs,
bereft of a reason to live—
Hear our prayers.

Tender Jesus, moved with compassion
for the sorrowing—
teach us the work of prayer.
Such prayer chases loneliness into the bosom
of Your love.
Meet these hurting ones in their lives,
dry their eyes and show them their duty.

Tender Jesus, teach us the perseverance
of prayer in the face of a
silent heaven

When you ask us to wait awhile for the answers
to our petitions.
See us—
those who would
see You smile and
feel Your hand of blessing.
Touch awake faith in a Father who cares:
A Father who will never reject us and is active on our behalf
Oh Lord, teach us the patience of unanswered prayer!
Thank You, God
Thank You, Jesus,
Thank You, Holy Spirit . . .
for Your love enabling,
for each other, and for the priceless
opportunity and privilege of prayer
partnerships.
Amen.

CHRISTMAS HEARTBEAT

Long Ago and Far Away

*

Long ago and far away in England, it was Christmas. My husband was 3,000 miles away in America, and our three little ones and I were reaching over the miles in thought and prayer to touch "Daddy." It was hard when he was away from us, but the children had never known anything else. I explained to them that Daddy was away because of Christmas. "Jesus, too, had to leave His family at Christmas. He didn't get home again for thirty-three years," I reminded them. I stirred the fire and settled down to read the children the Christmas story.

"That must have been awful for Jesus," said David thoughtfully, following my comment. "Why didn't He just come for a year or two?"

"It took thirty years to grow up from a baby to a man," I answered simply. "He chose to do it the hard way."

"He must have been lonely for His Daddy, like we are," Judy offered.

"Why couldn't He go back to visit?" Peter wanted to know.

We talked about it and were glad Jesus understood what we felt. "He left home for us so He could die for us," I explained. "Now He asks some of us to leave our homes for Him in order to tell people about it. Don't you think we should be *really* proud He chose our daddy to do that very important thing for Him?" I asked those three precious little upturned faces.

"I'm really proud!" said Peter.

"So am I," echoed the others.

"Me, too," I added—and meant it.

Room in My Inn

*

Another Christmas at Capenwray! Capenwray Hall is a beautiful castle-like building in England where the Briscoe family lived and worked with young people. The Christmas house party was always packed and was our responsibility. It meant lots of long hours and hard work. But there was plenty of fun to be had, too. The children loved to join in all the noisy games and lively meetings, mixing freely with the hundreds of youngsters from many different cultures who had come to be with us at this special time of year.

"This is what it must have been like that first Christmas," Stuart laughingly said to the kids. "There was no room at the inn then, and there's no room at the inn now!"

"We haven't put Jesus in the stable, though," said Judy.

"No, He is in the center of everything we do here," responded her daddy, "and He must always be!"

I thought about that and wrote a few verses to remind myself
to make sure He was in the right place in my life—not only at
Christmas but every day of the year!

Room in my inn for my business affairs,
Room in my inn for my worries and cares,
Room in my inn for the drink and the smoke,
Room for the act, for the off-color joke,
Room for my family, room for my wife,
Room for my plans, Lord, but no room for Your life,
And room for depression, when the party's all through,
Room for myself, Lord, but no room for You!
Room in my stable, Lord, room out of sight,
Room in the darkness and room where it's night,
Room with the cattle, the pigs, and the sheep,
Room where a newborn babe can't get to sleep;
Room with the dirt, Lord, the rats and mice,
Room with the maggots and room with the lice.
Room, you can have it, how generous am I—
I like to be good when my Savior comes by;

Room in the filth and the mire of my sin,
Room on the Cross my redemption to win,
Room in my stable but no room in my inn!

Afterwards

*

Obedience is doing without the angel,
doing the right thing by faith,
because you know it's right.
Doing it,
without the feelings—
Luke says, "then the angel left her . . ."
BUT JESUS HAD COME TO STAY!
Wasn't his name "IMMANUEL"?
I could imagine Mary
wondering why the angel disappeared!

"Where was the angel when I had to face
dear Joseph and tell him
I had met the God of Grace?
Oh, where was the angel when he wouldn't
listen to me and he called me
a liar, to my face?
And where was the angel who had promised me
protection . . .
Yet let Caesar call a census in the land?

And where was the angel when I needed
my sweet mother . . .
and nothing would work out as we had planned?
And where was the angel when we stood
before the rest house
and the keeper told us every room was taken?
And why were the angels talking to the shepherds
when I was in the cave and felt forsaken?
Where was the angel when I cried aloud
in childbirth,
And the Son of God was born upon this earth?
Oh, where was the angel when Herod's murderous soldiers
sought my baby boy
upon his birth?
Yet I didn't need to know the place of Gabriel's
appointment,
and I didn't need to hear the angels sing;
For marvelous though his person and wondrous
though his comfort,
'twas nothing to the presence of my King!
For *there* was the God of Grace when in the incarnation,
He visited my life and let me be

a part of His plan—of His high and
holy purpose as He lay within my
arms and let me see—
A face sweeter than the angels, and
softer than the sunshine and stronger far than
all the sons of light.

"Jesus Christ, my Savior, Immanuel, Redeemer,
The God of Glory, Majesty and Might!"

Choosing to Be Chosen

*

I'm sure God had chosen Mary to bear Jesus, yet He refuses to stop us human beings from choosing to be chosen! It's one thing to give God our Sunday attention or five minutes of devotional time, another to yield our bodies to do His will. Yet *we* live within our bodies and cannot serve Him without them! Didn't the Apostle Paul remind us about that?

> *Therefore, I urge you, brothers, in view of God's mercy,*
> *to offer your bodies as living sacrifices,*
> *holy and pleasing to God—*
> *this is your spiritual act of worship.*
> Romans 12:1

Presenting our bodies is part of our spiritual worship. My husband defines a body as "an earthly vehicle whereby a spiritual entity gets around in a physical environment." God dignified the human body by gifting it with divinity. Mary teaches us that we need to yield all of ourselves—body, mind, and spirit—to Him.

How many Marys, Lord, were there?
How many times did you try?
How often did Gabriel venture
Through the myriad stars of the sky?
How many minuscule humans?
How many a devout little maid
Heard your request for a body
And answered you thus so afraid.
"My love, Lord, you have it.
My will, Lord, 'tis thine.
I, to mighty Jehovah, my worship assign,
But my body, my body, my body,
'tis mine!"

How many Marys, Lord, were there,
Till Gabriel found her at prayer?
How many angels in glory,
were wondrously envious of her?
And how did it feel, Lord, to see her,
And watch at your feet as she fell,
As she yielded her soul and her spirit
And gave you a body as well?

"My love, Lord, you have it.
My will, Lord, 'tis thine.
I, to mighty Jehovah, my worship assign.
And my body, my body, my body,
'tis Thine!"

A Royal Birth

"Behold, a virgin shall be with child,
and shall bring forth a son,
and they shall call his name Emmanuel,
which being interpreted is God with us."
Matthew 1:23, KJV

A Royal Birth,
God in embryo, growing to birth size
a baby boy became.
Wrapped in swaddling bands of grace
A light was lit in a bale of hay,
Setting the world on fire!

They called Him the carpenter's child
They say he was brought up on
Joseph's knees
playing with a piece of wood.

He went around healing people and
being kind to sinners.
Christ His name . . .

God in Galilean robes
dressed for battle . . .
met the devil—paid the price—
and won the war!

Royal birth!
Royal life!
Royal death!
Royal
Resurrection!

A Boy Was He

*

Yet Jesus not only became a baby—He became a boy—

A boy was he
Yet very God of very God
A child,
yet wiser than his years
A boy was he
Yet very God of very God
The Lord's own Lamb appears.
A boy was he
Yet very God of very God
A carpenter's apprentice skilled.
A boy was he
Yet very God of very God
The Lamb His will fulfills.

Divinity breathing in air
with a boy's lungs:
Eternity eating a meal
with a boy's joy:

The Trinity coming to stay
in a boy's house,
in a boy's pain,
in a boy's world.

A boy was he
Yet very God of very God
A Son loved deeply by His own.
A boy was he
Yet very God of very God
The Lamb so far from home.

Divinity breathing in air
with a boy's lungs:
Eternity eating a meal
with a boy's joy:
The Trinity coming to stay
in a boy's house,
in a boy's pain,
in a boy's world.

Eminence contained
Immanence experienced

Holiness explained in a boy!
Truth read clearly,
Love loved dearly,
God known nearly
in a boy!

A boy was he
Yet very God of very God
A child, yet wiser than his years.
A boy was he
Yet very God of very God
The Lord's own Lamb is here!

Christmas Now

*

Can we think of a crib without a cross, or a cross without a crown? I think not. All are one, and one cannot be without the other two—or so it seems to me.

Straw Your throne,
cattle Your companions,
creatures made by Thee.
Jesus—birthed a man child.
King's crown left on Heaven's seat,
Cared for by a child
who hardly counts her age in double figures!
Poor,
scared,
not wanting to drop You
precious Baby King!

Hard the earth,
no other place to lay Your kingly head.
No need to count the stars—
You know their number.

They clapped their hands when You
created them,
Glad to shine then,
glad to shine now,
reminding You of home!

High Your cross where reigns death,
strange seat to share with such a monarch.
How is it that You take Your place
on such a bed of blood and pain?
For me, You say?
Straw Your throne?
Hard the earth?
High Your cross?
Cold Your grave?
For me?!

Cold the tomb of cruel reality!
Crying out in disbelief
to find itself so used.
Oh, regal Savior,
swathed in swaddling bands again

As in birth,
so in death,
Royal robes of wrath!

Hot the hell that welcomed You
Better far—the straw,
the earth,
the cross,
the tomb—than this!

A broken heart of love lies shattered
in this place.
A hideous smile of hate
twists Satan's face.
Remind me that my baby King
knew all of this
before He came in embryonic form.

Oh, thank You little King,
My Christmas
My Delight
My Joy

My All!
My party will be tinged with
tears of troubled thoughts,
as I gaze in Your manger bed:
Straw Your throne,
Hard the earth,
High Your cross,
Cold Your grave,
Hot Your hell!

Christmas now!
Great Your glory, Lord.
Reached Your Father down
Swaddling You in swathing bands of light;
You, who do delight His eyes—
Treasure of His heart!

Jesus, Jewel of heaven:
fire Your throne,
earth Your footstool now.
Empty cross and open tomb,
a witness to the hell

You overcame—
for Mighty King You are.

Straw Your throne,
Hard the earth,
High Your cross,
Cold Your grave,
Hot Your hell,

CHRISTMAS NOW!

He Laid It Down

*

It was time to emigrate to the U.S.A. Sell all the
furniture—and everything else—my husband told me. "It's
easier for the church leaders to provide us a home over there,"
he said. It seemed so easy at first—just sell everything. But it
wasn't. Some things, yes—but not *everything!* The wedding
presents, the special sentimental keepsakes, the children's toys
and dolls. We each had two cases—one for clothes, the other
for personal things. I found, to my horror, my fingers were
firmly gripping so much I had considered "yielded"—given!

"Release my fingers, Lord," I prayed. "Yes, help me to release
my grasp!" He helped me to let go then, as He has helped me
since. A little while back I wrote about that—at Christmas.
First I read Philippians 2:5-11 . . .

Your attitude should be the same as that of Christ Jesus:
Who, being in the very nature God,
did not consider equality with God something to be grasped,
but made himself nothing,
taking the very nature of a servant, being made in human likeness.

And being found in appearance as a man, he humbled himself
and became obedient to death—even death on a cross!
Therefore God exalted him to the highest place
and gave him the name that is above every name,
that at the name of Jesus every knee should bow,
in heaven and on earth and under the earth,
and every tongue confess that Jesus Christ is Lord,
to the glory of God the Father.

Then I spent time thinking about my clutching fingers and
wrote:

He came not trailing clouds of glory
He came not wearing heaven's crown
He left behind His father's golden city
And chose as birthplace Bethlehem's little town.

Equality with God was His by nature
And worship by the angels was His right
The honor due Him by His heavenly Father
He left to come and save us Christmas night.

He laid it down, He laid it down
And taking human form became a man,
He laid it down, He laid it down
And chose instead the world's redemptive plan.

So who am I to seek the world's dim glory
And who am I to fight for worldly crown?
What right have I to choose to work in city
In rural country or in tinsel town?

And who am I to grasp some vain ambition
Or who to choose a partner for my days?
Am I superior to the Christ who saved me
Do I have rights to keep or give away?

I'll lay them down, I'll lay them down
And make Him Lord of all I want to be
I'll lay them down, I'll lay them down
Lay hold instead of all He wants for me!

Lion of Judah

*

What a mystery! Meekness and Majesty! The Lion—yet the Lamb—how can this be?

Lion of Judah, great I AM,
yet Son of God and gentle Lamb;
The One who made all human life,
yet babe in womb of Joseph's wife.
Majestic One who naked came
to dress Himself in human shame.
Naked twice—in crib, on cross,
Lord of all who suffered loss.
Lion of Judah, great I AM
yet Son of God, and gentle Lamb.

Lion of Judah, great I AM
yet Son of God, and gentle Lamb;
Powerful voice of God most high
limited to baby's cry.
Mighty Father from above

needing now a mother's love.
Helper, hope of Israel,
helpless now Immanuel.
Lion of Judah, great I AM
yet Son of God and gentle Lamb!

Lion of Judah, great I AM
yet Son of God and gentle Lamb.
Majesty displayed in space
lets me look into His face;
meekness brings you near today
a Christmas babe in trough of hay.
A mighty God—a tiny child,
Omnipotence so meek and mild.
Lion of Judah, great I AM
yet Son of God and gentle Lamb!

Lion of Judah, great I AM
yet Son of God and gentle Lamb
came to Joseph, shepherd, king,
to those who needed songs to sing;

So hurting women, broken men,
could find new life—be born again;

Because of Him, the gentle Lamb,
Lion of Judah—great I AM!

EASTER HEARTBEAT

Easter

Easter brings such wealth of
imagery to mind
dear Lord—

A cross and pain
A grave and death
A stone pushed aside
by angels' touch to let the
sunshine in and
to let Thy Son stride
out—
rising with healing in His
wings.

In this quiet moment we pause
choosing our own
particular imagery that
helps us most to focus on
Your incredible sacrifice for us

and the meaning
of Easter

We thank You for bruising
the serpent's head
at Calvary
And yet half dead, and well on
the way to his doom, we still see
the snake in our world today
viciously devising
ways to hurt
Your people, Your church.

So we pray for the leaders of that
church worldwide
and for local
preachers, teachers, and witnesses
of truth
who are busy telling the whole story
to the whole world.
Oh, that Your children
would appropriate Your

victory over the
devil and be helped to
share the good news effectively.

Amen.

Scourged My King

*

My husband stopped me at the door of our room. "Jill, why don't you say something to the folks tomorrow, when we visit 'the pavement'?" I looked at him dumbstruck. We were taking a group of people around the Holy Land, and the following day we actually would stand on the stones that were believed (with good reason) to be the very ones where Jesus was scourged. What could I say? And how could I even get it out of my mouth? I, however, nodded and muttered that I'd think of something. That night, alone, I read the account of Jesus' trial and scourging in John 19:1-3:

Then Pilate took Jesus and had him flogged.
The soldiers twisted together a crown of thorns and put it on his head.
They clothed him in a purple robe
and went up to him again and again, saying,
"Hail, king of the Jews!"
And they struck him in the face.

I asked God for some little glimpse of what happened, that with my little mind and little words I might try to talk about

the biggest atrocity ever—the men God made playing games
with Him, even games of torture.

It was almost impossible to speak the next day without tears
coursing down my face. Kneeling on those precious stones I
offered God praise—and my poem.

Scourged my King, a plaited crown,
Runs the blood of Godhead down?
Ripped the flesh, the beard pulled out,
Cruel this sport and rude this shout.
Scourged my King, a plaited crown,
Runs the blood of Godhead down?

Scourged my King in soldier's den
Exposed to beasts that dressed like men,
Smelt the blood of prey soon caught,
Set my Jesus all at naught!
Scourged my King and fool of made,
God in heaven, what price you paid.

And all because of my heart's need
Sinful thoughts and sinful deeds.

A dirty soul, that dirtied Thee
On bloodied earth, on bloodied tree.
Scourged my King, a plaited crown,
Runs the blood of Godhead down?

Scourged my King, a plaited crown
Here I kneel a-trembling down,
Beat my fists in silent fury
While my world ignores your story.
Scourged my King, a plaited crown,
Runs the blood of Godhead down?

Scourged my King, a plaited crown,
Runs the blood of Godhead down?
Can I doubt your Father's loss
Broken God on broken cross.
Do I bear wound, or scar in me
That mirrors thine on Calvary?
Scourged my King, a plaited crown,
Runs the blood of Godhead down.

Easter Prayer

*

Two thousand years ago You came into Jerusalem
in humility, Lord—
Just as You come into
our world today
You stooped to conquer then
and You stoop to conquer now
by coming into our little lives—our miniature
moments.
People welcomed You then and
people welcome You
now—
little realizing accepting
You as Savior
means accepting Your cross
as well

Because You came as
lowly King
we can reign in life with You
but not without the cross.

The shadow of Your cross must mark us out of
the generic pack.
Stamping us with integrity
and acts of self sacrifice, mirroring
Calvary love.

May our selfless service
say to a watching world
"The cross is our abiding place."

We pray for the people—in this
church, dear Lord,
working daily in full view
of those who know not the
shadow of Your cross.
May we alert them
to the incredible price You paid
for their souls.

And we pray for the activities of this fellowship,
for teachers teaching, preachers preaching,
singers singing, pray-ers praying,
care-ers caring

May all the ministries know
the impact of Your presence!
Force us to re-assess
our attitudes, appropriate Your power
and live daily unto You,
Lord Jesus,
bringing everything
under the scrutiny
of the cross.

We pray for the sick and the suffering:
for missionaries and for those
who reject our Christ
on the mission fields of this globe,
and ask for the rain of revival to fall.
We pray for those who perpetrate violence
and those who are
recent victims of it, asking that
You stay the rapist, intervene when life
is threatened and make our
city a safer place in which to live.

So hear us, Lord,
and answer our requests
according to Your will.
May our praise and prayer this Easter season
gladden Your heart and make
Your sacrifice worthwhile!

Amen.

Judas

*

Oh silver things that bought His death
What, cry you out in disbelief
to be so used—to take His breath;
to buy His blood? Oh God of grief!
The scarlet cast of this my greed
gleams in my dark despair today;
It lights the serpent's sure approach
I cannot, cannot look away!
I kissed Him then, He called me friend,
for what—A cold, hard silver thing?
Well, now the tree waits Yahweh's child,
and winter takes the place of spring!

When Judas . . . saw that Jesus was condemned,
he was seized with remorse and
returned the thirty silver coins to the chief priests and the elders.
"I have sinned," he said, "for I have betrayed innocent blood."
"What is that to us?" they replied. "That's your responsibility."
So Judas threw the money into the temple and left.
Matthew 27:3-5a

Why Couldn't She Use

*

But one of his disciples, Judas Iscariot, who was later to betray him,
objected, "Why wasn't this perfume sold
and the money given to the poor? It was worth a year's wages."
John 12: 4-5

Why couldn't she use—
cheap oil
clean towels
a bowl of water
like anyone else?

She could have used cheap oil;
spikenard is worth a small fortune.

She could have wiped His feet
with common towels.

Long, thick hair unbraided in
such a wanton way

gives wrong impressions to
the watching men.

Such love should not be
spilled upon a rabbi's feet—
Such waste!
Cheap oil—she could have used
cheap oil and common towels.

And what's amiss with water in a bowl?
Tears belong in private places,
never shed in public show
upon a face exposed in grief,
that somehow finds relief—

Why couldn't she use cheap oil
common towels and
a bowl of water
like anyone else . . .

Like me, for instance!

Poor Mary!

*

It was Easter Sunday morning. Sitting in our lovely sanctuary, my heart filled to overflowing. I thought about the difference two days had made to my spirit. Good Friday had been such a *down* day as we tried to observe it for Him. But now it was over, and I captured a tiny little part of the relief. I loved Jesus so very, very much, and suddenly I was crying and saying to Him, "I'm so glad, dear Lord—so very, very glad that it's all over for You!" Did I catch a little of Mary's feelings?

Poor Mary! She knew He was dead; she'd watched Him die,
Hanging between the earth and sky.
She knew He was dead; she'd heard Him scream
As the filth of our sin had come between
Himself and His God, as the punishment rod
Fell to chastise His choicest prize.
She knew He was dead, so pardon her
For thinking Him only the gardener!

He called her name; He was just the same,
Save the holes in His hands and His spear-pierced frame.

The love and fire in His eyes were too much,
The strength and the thrill of His risen-life touch.
Dear Lord! Dear Lord! Oh, pardon her
For thinking You only the gardener!

Many folks that I know have a Jesus of gloom,
Alive, yet confined to His garden tomb.
Yes He came alive, but was never the same,
He never called them by their very own name!
He lives in His tomb and He tends to His grave,
Confined and helpless to seek and to save.

Look into His face, let go of His feet,
Stop trying to wrap Him in that winding sheet!
He isn't the gardener, a ghost, or a fake,
He's Rabboni, your Master and He rose for your sake.

— Round a Hammer in the Grass —

Did you ever wonder where the snake was when Jesus was on
the cross? I did.

Round a hammer in the grass—a snake lies
crass—
mouth open
forked tongue busy,
smiling.

Lewd men gape
purity raped hangs bare,
splayed out
on a stake of
splintered wood.

His nerves shivering, quivering,
tearing,
bearing the
weight of the hate of God

against Him
because of our sin.

Jesus suffers; frying His flesh
in the sun;
blood and mucous in His hair,
flies feasting
round His mouth—
His eyes—
Jesus dies!

Naked came He to us—
helpless then,
helpless now;
bound then,
bound now;
crying then, crying now.
"Where are you, Father?"
and way back when, as now—
then—coiled round itself
a viper—all intent,

hell bent
was smiling.

And so Christ dies a death of dread
while round his head
a crown of thorns—
and other things
weigh heavy on His mind!
Redemption
busy with His Father's work
expires for humankind.

The serpent ill concealed
could not prevent
our God, revealed in Christ,
from washing our world with His blood.

So—
Who smiles now, oh snake—
Oh, wicked Lucifer—
Oh, father of the night,
Appolyon, reptile,

vilely dressed
up tight inside your scaly
skin of horror?

God's Christ is safe,
and heaven is ours because of Him!
God smiles,
yea
laughs on Easter morn
as angels roll the
stone
on top of you!
For He whose death
bruised all your head,
waits patiently,
resting his heel in heaven!
Knowing
that His resurrection life
will be your doom.

God smiles
and so do we.

Oh, death,
where is your sting?
Oh, grave,
your victory!

The Breeze Too Grieved

*

A missionary friend wrote me a note. She had been walking in a particularly unpleasant part of town—near the garbage piles. She stopped when she caught sight of an orchid—yes, an orchid—that had taken root and was actually growing right on top of the very worst heap of stinking refuse. "Only God can grow an orchid on a garbage pile," she wrote.

A few years later as I thought of Jesus on the cross, her comment came to mind. Truly Jesus is God's prize flower.

The breeze too grieved to blow sighs
The grass ashamed to grow dies
Where crooked twists its God.

Light shuts its eyes in fear
The darkness gladly here
dresses its Maker's nakedness in shame's shadows.

The graves break
The rocks quake
Convulsed with compassion
emptying themselves
like Him . . . like Him.

But there strange thing—amid the cosmic clash
among the city's trash
Where once the cross loomed—
an orchid bloomed!
See nature smile,
For only God can grow an orchid on
a garbage pile
Now seeing God it was upon the tree
lest I should die,
The carpenter's hands nailed to my punishment
tell me of love as love is—
HIS!

Oh, precious Orchid—plucked by God
for Heaven's halls
on Easter Sunday morning—

Freshen our lives with your fragrance
Brighten our minds with your love.

Blossom on the trash pile of our lives
—in our confusion—
Jesus be our joy
making our desolation smile;
For who but you, Oh God—can grow
an orchid on
a garbage
pile!

Resurrection Life

*

Thank You, Lord Jesus, that Your death on the
cross made us fit for heaven,
and Your resurrection life
makes us fit for earth.

Because You live we can by Your grace
become partakers of Your divine nature.

Your life in us gives us God
in the garden of our lives,
meeting us even among the weeds.

Lord, some of us, like Mary, have wept
till we can weep no more;
and some like Peter and John
find it hard to believe there
is hope at all.

Greet us today with Your great glad
cry of triumph!

Help us to trust Your power to
raise us
above ourselves and our
circumstances—
and our sin.

And . . . send us on our way celebrating Easter
in our hearts, our lives and
our families . . .
We offer You now ourselves first for
Your service, then our offerings
as a token of our praise and
of our love . . .

for His sake, Who died and rose again,
even Jesus,

Amen.